D1074779

ALSO BY DAVID YOUNG

POETRY
At the White Window
Night Thoughts and Henry Vaughan
The Planet on the Desk: Selected and New Poems

NONFICTION
Seasoning: A Poet's Year

TRANSLATIONS
The Poetry of Petrarch
The Clouds Float North: The Complete Poems of Yu Xuanji
The Book of Fresh Beginnings: Selected Poems of Rainer Maria Rilke
Intensive Care: Selected Poems of Miroslav Holub
Five T'ang Poets
The Duino Elegies: A New Translation

CRITICISM
Six Modernist Moments in Poetry
The Action to the Word: Style and Structure in Shakespearean Tragedy
Troubled Mirror: A Study of Yeats' "The Tower"
The Heart's Forest: Shakespeare's Pastoral Plays
Something of Great Constancy: The Art of "A Midsummer Night's Dream"

BLACK LAB

BLACK LAB

David Young

ALFRED A. KNOPF   NEW YORK   2006

THIS IS A BORZOI BOOK
PUBLISHED BY ALFRED A. KNOPF

Copyright © 2006 by David Young

All rights reserved. Published in the United States by
Alfred A. Knopf, a division of Random House, Inc., New York,
and in Canada by Random House of Canada Limited, Toronto.

www.randomhouse.com/knopf/poetry

Knopf, Borzoi Books, and the colophon are registered trademarks of
Random House, Inc.

Library of Congress Cataloging-in-Publication Data
Young, David, [date]
    Black lab / David Young.—1st ed.
        p.   cm.
    ISBN 0-307-26322-3
    I. Title.
    PS3575.O78B55 2006
    811'.54—dc22   2005044301

Manufactured in the United States of America
First Edition

For Georgia

Contents

One

WALKING AROUND RETIRED IN OHIO

After Lu Ji

I wake up at dawn these days,
called by an unknown voice,
heart racing,
get up and dress, then hesitate—

there isn't anywhere I have to go!

—

Think of a recluse living in a gorge:
he spends a morning picking watercress,
sits on a hill to watch the sunset . . .

branches above him, clouds above the branches,
kingfisher green, kingfisher blue,
wind shouldering through honeysuckle
and you lose yourself in fragrance . . .

the small creek bubbles, slightly pensive,
echoes back from the ridge . . .

—

Wealth is absurd and fame's a filthy habit.
People who chase these things are addicts.

Joy can't be faked. Joy is just *there,*
was there all along, unscrolled itself

when you lost your urge to control
the many systems you would never master.

—

Get out of your car. Here's the Wildlife Preserve,
floating and humming with life.

The great big day, the new one.
Pines. Geese. A quizzical raccoon.

Weeds, clouds, birdsong, cicada buzz.
Now, let the weather lead you. Walk!

1.

Churchill called his bad visits from depression
a big black dog. We have reversed that, Winston.
We've named him Nemo, no one, a black hole
where light is gulped—invisible by night:
by day, when light licks everything to shine,
a black silk coat ablaze with inky shade.
He's our black lab, wherein mad scientists
concoct excessive energy. It snows,
and he bounds out, inebriate of cold.
The white flakes settle on his back and neck and nose
and make a little universe.

2.

It's best to take God backward; even sideways
He is too much to contemplate, "a deep
but dazzling darkness," as Vaughan says.
And so I let my Nemo-omen lead me
onward and on toward that deep dark I'm meant
to enter, entertain, when my time comes . . .
The day wheels past, a creaky cart. I study
the rippling anthracite that steadies me,

the tar, the glossy licorice, the sable;
and in this snowfall that I should detest,
late March and early April, I'm still rapt
to see his coat so constellated, starred, re-starred,
making a comic cosmos I can love.

My father's breathing chugs and puffs and catches,
a slow train slowing further, rattling in
to its last stop, a locked and shuttered station.

Ninety-nine years this pair of lungs, this heart,
have done their work without complaint.
Time now to let them stop and draw their wages.

The years slide down a chute and disappear;
as memories dissolve and vaporize,
the body simplifies to mottled matter,

and if the myths have got it right for once,
he turns to find a welcome somewhere else,
to touch my mother's face and make her smile.

PUTTING MY FATHER'S ASHES IN THE CEMETERY AT SPRINGVILLE, IOWA

August 7, 2003

My brother and my sister shade their eyes
against the noonday glare. My cousins stroll
among the graves. These Grant Wood hills,
rich now with corn and soybeans,
seem to be just the place to set
this marble shoebox
deep in the earth, next to my mother's,
this earth that's full of relatives:
grandparents, uncles, aunts, the infants too,
some that lived long enough for names, some not,
each generation giving ground to others,
hidden and peaceful, like the family farms
down at the end of narrow shaded lanes
where tractors doze and trees stand tall and green
dreaming the summer into autumn.

It was October, there was steady drizzle,
small mice were nesting in the buckskin grass,
maybe a chicken hawk was cruising overhead,
or just a magpie posted on a fence. . . .

I used to wonder why the Chinese poets
stopped off at battlefields, and mused, and wept,
picking up arrowheads and shattered halberds,
brushing quick poems on the hard-packed sand—

but I have been to Waterloo, and Gettysburg,
and come to think of it that beach in Normandy
named for the stockyard city I grew up in.
The great West, all those plains and badlands,

those miles of rye and soybean broken by a silo,
is neutral, sometimes, even to the magpies,
and maybe even mice can sense Wyoming
is mostly undulating empty prairie

and cloudscapes almost past conceiving.
Seeing the Tetons I couldn't quite believe
them, their weird beauty. It's slow work,
this hammering out our human world of spirit.

Like a soft doll the raptured angel lolls
above the dusty crèche; lights flicker
in all the downtown trees, while carols
crisscross the air from boxy speakers.

I'm in two places now: my country,
where the Nativity is clumsy but familiar,
and that inept museum, east of Nervi,
which shows me crèches of another order:

elaborate pageants, carefully arranged,
all lace and straw and flat-out piety,
the underside of what made art both strange
and wonderful, that Catholic sense of deity.

We're never going to get God right. But we
learn to love all our failures on the way.

EATING A RED HAVEN PEACH IN THE MIDDLE OF AUGUST IN OHIO

I'm having a tingle, a kind of
Wanda Landowska moment here,
as my senses converge on this fruit and the sun
rests a warm palm on my back and neck
and just for a moment I don't even mind
the bad news I've been hearing, reading,
the little daily shit storm, constant rain of lies,
the President's moral hairspray,
the weeds that riot though my herbs,
the distances to China and Peru.
                       They say
biting a fruit cost us our chance
to stay in Paradise? Well, Eve, old thing,
this peach, this perfume turned to wine
and all-out fuzz-bound sweetness
just sent me back there for a moment.

The way day inches up, off to the south,
grudging the world even a night-light's glow,
recalls an empty shop, its goods ransacked.

A day with a catch in its throat,
maybe a sob. Maybe a marsh
freezing slowly, like an empty dance floor.

The wind, that blowhard, has retired,
leaving us just the rolled steel cold
that chills our tears, fixes our angry smiles.

Seventeen starlings are desperately
searching an old lady's driveway
in case there are crumbs to fight for,

as the year groans on its hinge
and I start to hum for it all
since somewhere else, I think,

in a time and place much like this
my mother is teaching me carols
at a modest piano, next to an evergreen.

The fox paused at the field's edge, paw raised,
looked back and switched her tail, the way
a thrush will flutter among maple leaves—
that's when I thought of you, choosing
your words, taking your careful steps,
sleeping so restlessly.
Our distance is not so much miles
as years and memories, mine such leafy compost
I shake my head, too full of duff and humus
to get a bearing or a fix. Fox fire, that weird
by-product of wood decay, pulses in me today . . .
And look: after the vixen left, trailing a faint rank scent,
a freight passed slowly, flatcars in mizzling rain,
some of them loaded with truck trailers, some not,
objects that no more need attention than you need
waste time upon my lurching, coupled feelings.
Go with the fox—I send a sort of blessing
as gulls lift off the reservoir and day,
a spreading bruise against the western rim,
drains January and the freshened year.

Two

Thus we understand "cut" in the sentences "The barber cut my hair,"
"The tailor cut the cloth," and "The surgeon cut the skin" quite
differently because we bring to bear on these sentences a large cultural
background knowledge . . . For the same reason we don't know how to
interpret the sentences "Sally cut the sun" or "Bill cut the mountain."

—JOHN SEARLE

1.

Sally cut the sun,
Billy cut the mountain;
Andy had some fun
At the soda fountain.

Ruby caught the light—
No one told her not to;
Janice was a fright
After she'd been taught to.

Diamond cut the glasses,
Jesus cut the cheese;
Goat-boy cropped the grasses
Nodding in the breeze.

2.

Sally cut the sun,
Then she cut the moon;
She was carving paper
During the monsoon.

Billy cut the mountain,
Then it had a notch.
Sun went down behind it.
Billy drank some scotch.

Daniel handled language,
John observed him closely;
Breakfast was an anguish,
Dinner also, mostly.

Cyril toasts his mother,
Crystal coats a sleeve;
Talking with another
Makes me start to grieve.

Rose inside the iceberg,
Ice inside the rose.
Billy kisses Sally,
Sally breaks his nose.

Bill clear-cut the mountain.
Then it was all stumps.
Sally cut the sunlight,
Then she got the mumps.

Watch the phoenix rise
Perfect from its ashes,
Rigid with surprise
Circled round with flashes.

to remind us
that things change
into other
things

I look down
at my hand
turned to
hoof

it seems right
that my ears
lengthen,
grow fur

when a dog
can turn into,
say,
a cow

then March,
with
its good old
lion-and-lamb

act shouldn't surprise
us; we knew,
always,
how things

grow strange, merge,
trade features,
bray, moo,
roar, bleat . . .

LUNAR ECLIPSE GNOSTIC HYMN

> *Dozing on horseback,*
> *The far moon in a continuous dream,*
> *Steam of roasting tea.*
>
> —BASHŌ

All of us missed the total eclipse
because it was overcast all night,
clouds hiding the great event as if we were
deep under water. That was a kind of
eclipse as well,
from one point of view,
gigantically complete, with the fat moon
hovering somewhere far above
in its own sea of moonlight
just not the one we had hoped for, a big
kohlrabi sliding into the shadows, or a
lumpfish swimming out of sight,
maybe the moon-round blushing like a bride,
newly naked before her groom,
opening,
perfect in her own way,
queen of the night,
reciprocity personified,
stone maiden of a billion years,
Tuxedo Junction's momma,
understanding us at last

vivacious and alone,
walking wheel, tu-
xedo junction
yes, please tell my future, Madame
Zelda!

Socrates says that trees have nothing to teach us. And with that, the fall begins, the human fall from grace. A fall the trees could, of course, teach us about.

Plato can have a dialogue with his own texts; he writes them out, he studies them, he has more thoughts; the process now has its own momentum. Who needs trees? Who needs winds to breathe with, streams to enter and converse with? We fall from the world into language, a delicate, inexorable prison.

I babble, therefore I am, thinks Descartes, a little later. Beyond his window, the world fades away, flattening and draining. Leaves stop talking; tongues are the only tongues.

This labyrinth, this mental forest stocked with non-trees. Memories are stalking me, thinking's a walkabout. I raise my hand within my mind and wave. To what?

The trees are full of life, streamlined and shapely;
their leaves are blobs and networks, rising water,
and everything is bluish green, as if
this whole scene were submerged.

The two men, shapely too, have one strong contrast:
the younger poet's arms are at his sides,
palms out, a gesture of rejection.

Virgil, however, holds both arms aloft,
not just referring to the forest but
by being treelike, even more than Dante,
he's saying, Blake insists,
We are the forest!

It is not other, it is what we are!
The trees lean in to listen and agree.

WURFSCHEIBE, mit
Vorgesichten besternt,

wirf dich

aus dir hinaus.

1.

THROWPLATE, with
a face full of stars and foresights

throw yourself

out of yourself.

2.

THROWNDISC
starred with ancestor faces,

throw thyself

out of thyself.

3.

DISCUS, starred
with prehistoric things to come

go
throw

yourself
out.

4.

FRISBEE,
premonition-constellated—

spin right on

out of yourself.

5.

NIGHTSKY, you discus,
stellate with foreseeings,

toss

thyself

away.

6.

BIGBANG, a mix
of faces, warnings, stars,

finish it

be the Big
Crunch.

ANOTHER GNOSTIC HYMN

Although the project seemed to have a purpose,
buying time (something I guess we all do),
cold looks came from your mirror, time and again,
dark depths you saw ahead and past your shoulder:
easy to feel distress, even for optimists.

Fantastic moments hovered in your memory,
going brighter and then dimmer as you slid toward sleep,
holding out hope for a day without depression
in turn extending to a week, a month, a year,
just when you thought you were stuck in time's waiting room
kindly and lost and bereft,
longing for someone, even perhaps your mother, who would
make it less lonely and bewildering,
never to have to say you were hopeless again
or ask a favor you knew you wouldn't get,
powerless, reduced to begging,
questioning even your own right to exist.

Reveries get interrupted, don't they?
Sailboats cross the horizon,
trains hoot at night, disappearing west,
under and over highways filled with trucks,

ventriloquists of absolution while
we weep and pace around the crossroads where
x marks the spot, the place that someone died—
younger than she should have been, by now the pretty
zombie of somebody's dim imagination.

I grabbed the doorknob and it burned my hand.
The door was frozen shut in that much heat.

"And this is how you die . . ." I dropped down flat
and slithered toward the door to the garage.

That's where they found me, curled up like a fetus,
most of my arm skin burned away, not worth

reviving, truly. In the ambulance,
I said it best: "Please, God, don't let me live."

I do burn cases now, a plastic surgeon;
when they first ask about my waffled skin

I know they're going to make it. I explain
about my grafts, how thighs and butt and groin

supplied the stuff that covers arms and hands.
I don't detail how many operations.

They start to think of life, of coming back.
I do not tell them, though, because they know,

that when you've been to hell, a part of you
will always stay there, stopped at that hot door.

Tom goes by on his motorcycle.

I'd like to wave, but he's already disappeared over the hill. Tiny now . . . tiny Tom.

'Bye, Tom.

It's summer here, birds singing as the dawn expands from pearl gray to lemon yellow.

Dead poets show up at dawn.

Here's Miroslav, watching a spider build its web.

Here's Kenneth Koch, who died last week, sitting quietly, hands folded.

Here's Shahid, fixing his *ghazals,* obsessed with Kashmir, keeping suffering at arm's length.

Tom goes by on his motorcycle.

Three

The tiny spacecraft twists and burns, exploding
against the friction of the atmosphere,
raining small pieces over Texas.

If you could ride the tall auroras
dancing above the Pole, perhaps
you could exempt yourself from pain?

Oh wrap this up in language, quick,
so I can bear it. Talk about Icarus or Phaeton,
tell stories of our origins and hopes.

Grape-colored sky at evening—
the mind walks numbly over windblown acres
picking up tiles, fragments, chunks.

Every microcosm needs its crow,
something to hang around and comment,
scavenge,
alight on highest branches.

Who hasn't seen the gnats,
the pollen grains that coat the windshield—
who hasn't heard the tree frogs?

In the long march that takes us all our life,
in and out of sleep, sun up, sun gone,
our aging back and forth, smiling and puzzled,
there come these times: you stop and look,

and fix on something unremarkable,
a parking lot or just a patch of sumac,
but it will flare and resonate

and you'll feel part of it for once,
you'll be a goldfinch hanging on a feeder,
you'll be a river system all in silver
etched on a frosty driveway, you'll

say "Folks, I think I made it this time,
I think this is my song." The crow lifts up,
its feathers shine and whisper,

its round black eye surveys indifferently
the world we've made
and then the one we haven't.

I've made his amber aftershave last out
through this whole year of missing him;
I wear my father's cardigan.
I swear I'm turning into him,

saying "Yupyupyup" to the puppy
as I bend to leash him, breathing harder,
pursing my lips as memories crowd my head,
settling my hat on firmly as I leave.

The other day, though, on the icy creek,
as a heron rose up from a crosswise trunk
I slipped and slid against the snowy bank,
cracked through the ice sheet, up to one knee.

The dog looked rightly puzzled. As for Dad,
he'd not have been that dumb, I tell myself,
making my aging foolishness keep me
younger, somehow, and singular.

Midwinter here, a frozen pause, and now
some nineteen years since cancer took your life.

This month's old god, they say, faced opposite directions,
backward and forward. May I do that too?

It's much the same. Deer come and go, as soft
as souls in Hades, glimpsed at wood's edge toward dusk;
their tracks in daylight show they come at night
to taste my neighbor's crab trees, last fall's fruit
shrunk down to sour puckered berries.

And where, in this arrested world,
might I expect to meet your cordial spirit?

You would not bother with that graveyard, smooth
below its gleaming cloak of snow. You'd want
to weave among the trees, beside the tiny kinglet,
gold head aglow, warming itself
with ingenuities, adapting, singing,
borne on the major currents of this life
like the creek that surprised me yesterday again,
running full tilt across its pebbled bottom
even in this deep cold.

Sometimes I feel like one of the world's bad headaches.

—

Fallen persimmon, shriveled chestnut,
I see myself too clearly.

—

A huge cement truck turns the corner, and you get the full impact
of its sensuality.

—

Carrying the book of shadows a low moon
crosses the power stations the refineries. . . .

—

Geysers of light
that mate around cities.

—

The comet was in the closet. Shaggy and silent.

—

There's no dark side to this moon.
No light one either.

—

We have some quiet families in this neighborhood.
Constellations, let's start from there.

—

A codger watering his broccoli
talks up the art of gardening as
we gaze at his cabbages and gooseberries.

—

Sometimes we know we are part of a crystal
where light is sorted and stored.

—

When you get old you can read yourself,
in order not to repeat yourself. Advice
from a poet I used to know . . .

Dante has slipped and Virgil helps him up.
Or is it the other way around?
Exactly forty years today I married Chloe. . . .
So many who were there have left *this* world
and still I wish I could converse with them,
break bread, drink wine, taste cheese and honey,
tell them I miss them, say to them that my world
seems to get bigger as it empties out.

A thundershower flails the backyard trees;
a house finch perches, seeking thistle seed.

Let's rewrite Genesis, by God, admit
Eve must have given birth to Adam, then
he didn't want to be beholden to her,
made up a sky-god who would punish her.

We search, in slumber, like a clumsy diver
feeling his way along the ocean bottom,
looking for wreckage, treasure, coral,
looking to surface into sunlight—
that glass of water, sitting on the table,
where once again the panther comes to drink . . .

Virgil fell down and Dante helped him up.
Or was that too the other way around?

1.

Reading *The Secret Life of Dust,*
learning about
the "wispy disk" of cosmic dust
that circulates around the sun and that
"on rare occasions you can see
a glowing slice of this
'zodiacal light,' "
described by an astronomer
named G. Cassini, 1683,
I realize that I've seen it!

Way out above the sea, a shining wedge
we couldn't figure out as we came down
at dusk from our big climb
to Santa Croce.

We were so lost and tired that our view,
the *Golfo Paradiso* all spread out
from Genoa to Portofino mountain,
made hardly any sense,
although we had to venerate the sea
a sheet of hammered metal
in mute and muting light
as we stepped down the path

as carefully as pack mules,
hurrying to get back
to where we'd have
our bearings once again
before the dark closed in.

David, you said the odd
inverted pyramid with blurry corners
might be a UFO. Janine and I
thought it was some strange opening in clouds.
Well, now we know, we pilgrims,
who had been past the Stations of the Cross
going and coming, and had talked about
the pious folk who climbed up on their knees
on special days, at dawn,
up to that little church
that stands so high and barren. . . .

2.

Now we know what? That in a world
where superhuman meanings have been drained
we take our best encounters with the things
that are not human, don't belong to us,
the "zodiacal light" just one more sign
that points back to itself, or at the best
to its own cosmic history:
our origins in dust,
that cloud that once congealed
enough to form a star
that then became our sun
and then helped form the earth
and still rains down around us,

still lights up the sky,
a burning golden triangle
around the equinox
above the sea beyond
the port of Genoa.

Comets go past, and we don't notice,
asteroids just miss us by two moon lengths,
the sun burns on, throwing gigantic flares and flowers,
we fill our eyes and word-hoards,
pick our way down mule trails,
and trust that somehow we belong to this,
the life of secret dust,
and it makes sense, somehow.

I might have spoken to that glow.
"Oleh," I might have said. *"Grandfather."*

I might have fallen to my knees, for once.
Ashes to ashes. Secret life. And dust
and light, a little light,
is maybe all we have?

3.

I think I'd like to write
The Sacred Life of Dust,
but I don't have the means.
Parked along a back road,
I'm jotting all this down
on old prescription pads
and one much-crumpled shopping list,
a January day,
the sun a dimming disk;
the radio is offering
the best thing that could happen,
"Das Musikalische Opfer,"
Bach's canons that perform
like crabs, mirrors, comets,
and I'll go on about my errands now,
something for our dinner,
something from the pharmacy.

A blue jay soars up to an apple branch
in one unfolding movement
and I look on in shock,
as if I'd never seen
a living thing that flies!

Part of me stays on earth,
part of me rises with the jay.

The day rolls forward toward
the secret life of dusk.

Four

1. Poems in the Mountains

Every person has a weakness;
mine is writing poems;
I've cut most ties with life,
but still I keep this habit.
Each time I glimpse a vista,
each time I meet a friend,
I start to fashion stanzas, chanting
as though I'd seen a god.

Since I was banished here
I've lived up in the hills.
When I have done a poem
I climb the road to East Rock.
I lean on huge white stones
I swing from cassia branches.
My crazy singing wakes the hills and valleys:
the birds and monkeys all come out to look.
People might laugh to see and hear me do this;
it's better that the place is so deserted!

2. The Shoes

I was airing some clothes in the courtyard
and found a pair of shoes from my hometown.
Somebody gave these to me. Who?
That lovely girl who was my neighbor—
and now her words come back to me:
"Take these, and they'll be a sign
that we will start and end together,
moving through life just like this pair of shoes
stepping together, resting together."

Here I am now, in exile,
a thousand stormy miles and many years
away from her, that distant lover,
and all I have left is these shoes.

Nostalgia weighs me down all morning
as I stare at the shoes and fondle them.
I'm on my own. The shoes are still together.
But I will never pair with her again!

Well, I have got my share of tears and sorrow.
and this brocade's too delicate and fine
to stand the rain that murders every blossom:
the color's going to fade, and the silk flowers
are wilting even as I watch them.

3. The Cranes

The autumn wind has just begun to blow
and there goes the first leaf, falling.

The path is dry; I stroll it in my slippers,
wearing a padded coat against the cold.

The floods run off into the drainage ditches,
the light slants through the delicate bamboo.

Evening comes early; along a mossy path
the gardener's boy escorts a flock of cranes.

4. Dreams of Climbing

All night, in dream, I climbed a rugged mountain,
all on my own, with just my holly staff,
a thousand peaks, a hundred thousand valleys,
and in my dream I found my way to all
and all that time my feet were never sore—
I climbed with all the strength I had in youth.

When mind goes back in memory, does the body
also turn back into its younger self?
Or can it be, when body grows decrepit,
that soul can still be strong or even stronger?

Well, soul and body both are just illusions;
the same thing goes for dreaming and for waking.
By day my feet are tentative and feeble;
by night they take me springing through the mountains.
Since day and night take equal parts in life
maybe I'm gaining just as much as losing!

5. Last Poem

They've put my bed by an undecorated screen
and brought the stove in front of this blue curtain.

My grandkids read to me. I listen,
and watch the servant heating up my soup.

I sketch an answer to a poem from a friend,
and search my pockets, paying for my medicine.

When I have finished dealing with these trifles
I'll lie back on my pillow, face the south, and sleep.

What does it mean to say an aging man loves a younger woman? Phyllis is depicted riding around on Aristotle's back, in his study, among his books. He's happy, apparently, just feeling her warm fundament and full buttocks on his old back.

Emotional chaos, forming into an order of opposites: his humiliation, her indifference.

—

Why would he not love youth, love beauty, things he is not? We revisit our necessary energies by any means we can, hoping the visits are relatively harmless. The angel of age is a sleepy fellow, a shaggy woodman, a puked-out volcano.

Youth and beauty are such a headlong thrill when you don't possess them yourself.

And yet one feels ridiculous. "I don't wish to play Pantalone," said M, looking a little desperately at me.

—

A peach orchard stretches eastward from this point.

I walk with you often, even under icy skies. Fires smolder on some horizon.

And whoever drinks from this particular well can taste the underlying bitterness in its clear sweet water.

—

A darkened village and a careful stroll through, holding a lantern. If a shutter would swing wide and a hand and wrist appear, beckoning. But it's just a theater set, already being folded and carted off to storage.

—

A rock and another rock. And the name of this flower, is it aconite?

Mornings filling with birdsong. Even the gulls want to be musical, knifing through clustered mist, mewing.

And is the imagined mouth the one we really kiss? Can one kiss, innocently bestowed, flower forever, a moisture and softness that mollify the demon?

—

Simple visits together, one to a shop, one to a large open-air market. Two lunches. A brief look at a small room, neatly kept. A chair next to a window.

A bag of bay leaves, bought in a dark and fragrant emporium, gradually used up for cooking.

—

To take communion between your legs!

THE DREAM OF THE MOVING STATUE

Nothing much, and little else.
We had a lot of rooms to visit. Nothing simple.

We used a flashlight just to get around
the huge and cluttered building. No one spoke.

Clusters of trash and funny echoes;
something that moved ahead of us, a rat,

maybe a bat or one small roosting owl.
I hummed a tune that was inaudible

and you, you seemed morose, remembering
dead family members, pets you'd lost . . .

Well, nobody got hurt and no one minded
the pastness of the past, its growing distance.

This was the sort of thing we did at night,
often while sleeping, sometimes when awake.

VILLANELLE

We've only just met and I miss you already—
Distracted, I think of just you, only you.
I track you on surfaces. Where is your beauty?

I waited forever, millennia heady
With longing, skies black and skies blue.
We've only just met and I miss you already.

I've never lost hope in my waiting, my duty,
And it doesn't matter that I can't quite touch you.
I track you on surfaces. Where is your beauty,

What world has it gone to, to shelter its body,
And will it reward me for being so true?
We've only just met and I miss you already.

I feel like a mountain—that huge and that steady—
I feel that my mind is expanded and new.
We've only just met and I miss you already.
I track you on surfaces. Where is your beauty?

after Carlos Germán Belli

The flute players, two men, face each other. The virtuoso prince, his back to us, wears a strange peaked cap. The foreigner, whose beard and costume give him away (Mongolian?), faces us. His eyes are downcast as he concentrates on his playing.

The prince's robe is olive green. White, purple and red chrysanthemums, widely spaced, make up its ornamentation. The foreigner's robe is lavender. A bright red under-robe shows below. In the silence of the scene, costume and garb must replace the unheard music.

They are next to some kind of monumental gate. Is the virtuoso teaching? Welcoming a visitor? Is this duet a habit or an accident?

This prince is said to be so gifted that once, when he had been robbed, the sound of his flute in response to his loss made the thieves repent and return what they had taken.

The full moon takes it in and gives it back. The flutists almost float, like ghosts, in its disinterested sea. They mirror each other, playing together, silent and concentrated, alike within their differences. The moon will wax and wane, always the same because it is always changing.

Three crisscrossed daffodils
faint lamps in the rubble

where without any warning
I'm shattered by your absence

wondering will I always
blunder into this emotion

so large and mute it has no name
—not grief   longing   pain

for those are only its suburbs
its slightly distracting cousins—

summoned just now by these
frilled blossoms

butter yellow horns
on lemon yellow stars

indifferent   innocent
charging in place

advance guard of a season
when I will join you.

Inside my dream the fair-haired ancient saint
who visited a group of living friends
gathered together in an English cottage

walked without stepping, read our thoughts,
spoke without need to use his mouth,
shone with a glow that didn't hurt the eyes,

moved among those he blessed
smiling a riveting smile,
and felt, when he came to hug me,

not like another body but
not immaterial either, since
his fragrance was amazing.

When I was left alone in that dim room,
stroking a smoky cat and musing,
my mind charged up with wonder and relief,

it didn't seem to me I'd been "converted"
but it did seem I'd had a glimpse of something
that would remember me when I forgot it.

Dusk on these late winter days
is a matter of daylight giving a little shrug,
then vanishing.

But when it does, the blue snow moment comes.

That's when, for instance, two or three deer
materialize from nowhere, stroll through the backyard,
and vanish in the woods. As when the ancient gods
came down to wander their enchanted world.

Then I remember to breathe again,
and the blue snow shines inside me.

March 2005

Notes and Acknowledgments

"At the Little Bighorn" was partly inspired by Stanley Plumly's essay "The Abrupt Edge," in his *Argument and Song: Sources and Silences in Poetry.*

"Dawn on the Winter Solstice" is for Ruth Green and John Young.

"Faux Pas" is for Eugenio Montale and Elizabeth Antalek.

The John Searle quote that inspired "Sally and the Sun" appeared in a review in *The New York Review of Books.*

Gnostic hymns were sometimes abecedarian.

"Plato and the Fall" first appeared in *Meridian.*

A translation of the Celan poem by Katharine Washburn and Margret Guillemin, in *Paul Celan: Last Poems,* reads as follows: "DISCUS, / starred with premonitions, // throw yourself // out of yourself." I owe the last variation to a suggestion by Ray English.

"A Doctor's History" derives from a story in *The Cleveland Plain Dealer,* by Harlan Spector, about Dr. Mark McDonough, 7/2/01.

"Walking Home on an Early Spring Evening" first appeared in *The Laurel Review.* This poem is for Judy Karasik.

"Chloe in Late January" first appeared in *The New Yorker*. This poem is for Newell and Margaret Young, and for Franz Wright.

A cento is a literary composition formed by combining separate verses or parts of existing works.

"The Secret Life of Light" first appeared in *The Journal*. The book *The Secret Life of Dust* is by Hannah Holmes. This poem is for David Carlson and Janine Massard.

"After Bo Juyi: Five Poems of Old Age" first appeared in *CipherJournal*. Bo Juyi lived from 772 to 846 and spent the last thirteen years of his life in retirement, when he also wrote some of his best poems. These are free adaptations of his late work.

"Petrarch Watches the Moon Rise Over the Vaucluse" was first published in *Meridian*.

"The Dream of the Moving Statue" first appeared in *Smartish Pace*.

The villanelle by Carlos Germán Belli was introduced to me by my student, Renée Corrigan.

"Yoshitoshi" was first published in *Cue*. This artist's entire series of woodblock prints, "One Hundred Aspects of the Moon," also gave me inspiration. Each of Yoshitoshi's prints has the moon somewhere in it, visible or implied. I admire the virtuosity that commits itself to such a significant set of variations. This poem is for Tom Van Nortwick.

The saint in the dream described in "Swithin" was unidentified. I decided to call him Swithin because I liked that name. This poem appeared in *Meridian*.

Special thanks to Margaret Young, Judy Karasik, Charles Wright, David Walker, and Deborah Garrison for advice on assembling this manuscript.

A NOTE ABOUT THE AUTHOR

David Young has written nine previous books of poetry, including *At the White Window* (2000), and *The Planet on the Desk: Selected and New Poems* (1991). He is a well-known translator of the Chinese poets, and more recently of the poems of Petrarch and Eugenio Montale. A past winner of Guggenheim and NEA fellowships as well as a Pushcart Prize, Young is the Longman Professor Emeritus of English and Creative Writing at Oberlin College and an editor of the prestigious Field Poetry Series at Oberlin College Press.

A NOTE ON THE TYPE

The text of this book was set in Sabon, a typeface designed by Jan Tschichold (1902–1974), the well-known German typographer. Based loosely on the original designs by Claude Garamond (c. 1480–1561), Sabon is unique in that it was explicitly designed for hot-metal composition on both the Monotype and Linotype machines as well as for filmsetting. Designed in 1966 in Frankfurt, Sabon was named for the famous Lyons punch cutter Jacques Sabon, who is thought to have brought some of Garamond's matrices to Frankfurt.

Composed by Creative Graphics, Inc.,
Allentown, Pennsylvania

Printed and bound by United Book Press,
Baltimore, Maryland

Designed by Soonyoung Kwon